Create Your New Life of Abundance

Make a FULL financial recovery with a new money-attracting mindset

Jennifer Lancaster

ISBN-13: 978-0-9804112-9-4

Cataloguing-in-Publication data:
Creator: Lancaster, Jennifer (Jennifer Lee), 1971- author.
Notes: Includes bibliographical references.
Subjects: Finance, Personal.
Saving and investment.

Dewey Number: 332.024

Disclaimer: This book is written as an educational guide only and does not constitute financial or legal advice. While every effort has been taken to ensure all material is correct and up-to-date, the author accepts no legal responsibility for errors or omissions. Each individual's situation is different, and all readers should seek professional consultation before embarking on a financial plan. The author accepts no legal responsibil-ity for the performance of any budgeting tools suggested herein. The author does not receive any commissions or benefits from any organisa-tions mentioned.

Publisher: www.powerofwords.com.au/books
Published by Power of Words, Clontarf, QLD, Australia.

Please give feedback on the book wherever sold.

Dedicated to my Mum and Dad, the saver and the spender personality, who have managed to create a passive income in retirement.

Table of Contents

INTRODUCTION

Are you humbled with debt... or feeling alone in your money woes? If you've suffered a major setback in work or in business, no doubt you will, for a time, feel like a failure.

But why feel so alone, when anyone who has ever taken a risk in life has also felt the pang of failure. And if anyone you know hasn't failed big, then they're just not trying!

It's not just you who are in peril. You are not on a dry, deserted island in a sea of prosperity. The working and middle classes of Australia, Europe and the US toil away and spend heartily, unaware of their own possible health failings or redundancies in an unknown future.

Millions of us mortgage holders and personal borrowers are sitting in this tinny, tilting ship that may let the water in if things go wrong and our debt repayments begin to overtake our income. As of 2015, Australians led the world's developed nations in borrowing levels at 180%, while the UK softened their ratio to 150% and the US reined it in at 110%. Still too much debt for a secure future.

Over the past 25 years in Australia, the average mortgage debt has risen from 10 to 28% as a proportion of housing values.[1] Worryingly, a PIMCO study also found that Australians were being "irrationally exuberant" and borrowing too much to invest in housing, exposing the economy to financial shocks. This trend was catalysed by the 'line of credit' style mortgage packages introduced in the 1980s and 1990s, which are still available (with greater restrictions) today.[2]

In fact, with the marketplace offering every kind of credit, from quick little loans to cumbersome mortgages, it's easier than ever to get into money trouble.

So it seems the necessity for this book has never been greater, as people who have borrowed big come to realise that they simply cannot repay their debt, pay their regular bills, and still breathe. Having abundance means not stressing about money, to start with. Furthermore, it means having fun in life and attracting more!

MY STORY

I like to be prepared for any eventuality. So I look for flexibility in a loan product to cater for any life changes. In 2008 I researched broadly in personal finance to not only write a helpful book, but also to prepare ourselves for our first ever mortgage. Together for four years, my husband and I agreed on buying a house in an affordable region of Queensland, with sun, sea and sand.

With a deposit of 30%, a $20,000 cash buffer, and a flexible offset mortgage, yes I thought we had worked it all out perfectly. As we sailed along on recruitment business income, flying off to Europe, buying our house on mortgage and so on, we both thought the future was rosy.

In 2008, along came the GFC, businesses stopped hiring and my husband's recruitment business income plummeted to zero. As a side point, the managed funds we bought lost 40% of value, but we had to sell to pay for business costs. For two years we struggled on, with just that buffer and our wits to live on.

My husband works hard and is incredibly smart with technology (that's why he's with me, right?). He learned a whole new trade in graphic arts and started a web design business to bring in an income. But this didn't mean that his talent and communication skills were sudden, surefire elements of success, because there was an ingredient missing... something we will discuss in depth in this book.

At the time, I brought in a small income from copywriting, but I mainly focused on being a good mother and household manager. It was touch and go, budget wise.

One missing factor was:

We had not diversified our income.

Coming to the brink of financial disaster and contemplating selling our home was a big 'wake up call' for us. But it could have been much worse. If we had been maxing out credit cards, paying private school fees, paying car loans, and highly mortgaged without a buffer, we may well have gone from enjoying a nice house in a nice suburb to a crappy rented house and scraping along on welfare. I got rid of my credit card problem in 2002, and never got another.

As it was, we managed to hang in there with a flexible offset, some extended family gifts, and cutting back on non-essential costs. But it was hard, and all the stressors especially taxed our marriage.

WHAT ABOUT YOU?

Perhaps you're facing the brink of financial ruin right now, and you're desperate for a life preserver to stop you from drowning. Many people on the brink start looking for easy to get, high interest loans... that still don't cover all of their outgoings. Or they feel stuck and delay payments. Both only make their troubles worse, as these measures either delay the problem or increases interest payments, thus creating more pressure in the future.

Even if debtors are calling and demand notices are still coming, this period doesn't have to be the end of your financial story. This book is not about pitying or martyrdom. It's about how you can take positive steps, reduce stress, get support, and recover emotionally and mentally. Even if it's slow, things will gradually get better.

While it may seem that all your problems are external, the only way through to prosperous times is to first take a look inside yourself. If you always look outside yourself for those to blame, then this can come as quite a revelation.

So there is a challenge in this book – a challenge to bite back your pride, gather your courage, and take the actions that will secure your (and your family's) future and improve your outlook. When you look back on this period, you may even see the strength you pulled seemingly from nowhere and be immensely proud of yourself.

It's also wise, if you are presently earning an income, to prepare for any income drop, no matter from whence it comes. I like the saying: "expect the best but prepare for the worst".

I am just like millions of people. I had unfounded fears and poor beliefs… and for years I gave up halfway through, before success had time to catch up. I believed my lack of success was the fault of my partner and that motherhood held me back. Deluded, yes.

Through self-awareness and journalling, I realised how my mindset, limiting beliefs, and reacting to other people's opinions was blocking my way to success. The positive psychology and success books I read have given myself, and many others, hope for change.

A BREAKTHROUGH

While barely keeping afloat financially, I kept waiting until I had stability—whatever that is—and someone to guide me. One day I looked at all my half-finished projects, my dream goals, and I realised that it had to start with me. I had the power to change my circumstances through slowly changing my beliefs, and then taking action on my new beliefs.

I was going to damn well finish my unfinished projects, because nobody was coming along to say, "go on girl, you can do it".

The next book I finished and launched was *Power Marketing*, as small business marketing was on my mind. It helped attract businesspeople, to then ask what I could offer them in terms of services.

I started writing this book in 2011. Besides being more aware of my poor self-worth and my values, I also went to a spiritual practitioner. With a cleansing and energy healing, this woman somehow got rid of some subtle aspects that were blocking my success. She then guided me to discover my own destiny. (Subtle aspects are those elements in the non-material world that can be holding you back). In my minds' eye, I saw a hand turning the pages of a book and then I imagined looking out at an ocean horizon. Apparently, this means freedom.

Combining this with my knowledge of positive intention, I bit the bullet and put on book publishing workshops. After my non-existent book promotions and subsequent poor sales, it was a nice surprise to garner real interest. I now also help others to fulfill their publishing dreams within a budget.

Anthony Robbins says, "you've got to get yourself in a state of certainty (before you can get results)".

If you're tired of feeling uncertain and you're ready to push through until you feel successful, then let's keep going.

The first part of this book is about emotions and mindset and what you can do to improve any limiting beliefs.

The second part contains the 'how to prosper' in many practical ways. I call it 'the Seven Pillars of Financial Sense'.

Your recovery plan doesn't have to be carried out in a week. It's far better to take it one step at a time... build on small successes, learn from setbacks, and never, ever give up on your dreams.

PART ONE:

EMOTIONAL RESCUE

CHAPTER 1

CRISIS POINT

If you're suffering right now because of a job loss, business cash flow woes, or an expensive health crisis – you might not realise that there are actually two levels of problems to acknowledge.

The first is practicalities: not enough income to meet expenses, bill notices overflowing, partner wants a separation, the kids need new clothes and books, perhaps medical concerns and bills, and other realities of life. These things can all keep you awake at night, it's only human.

The second level of problems is emotional; it's the fallout from all of the above.

For your recovery, you will need the practical: better money management all-round, income boosters, and easier debt repayment options. And you'll also need the emotional and spiritual: self-help exercises, reading, maybe praying, and a counsellor or a wise friend's support.

EMOTIONS IN A MONEY CRISIS

You might wonder why you can't think of good solutions to your money problems right when you need it. It's probably because of the high level of emotional stress you and your dearly beloved are under. Fear, doubt and worry over your life can interrupt your normal idea creation and decision-making abilities.

It's a time when it's so easy to turn to distractions, alcohol, gambling, and every other vice in the book, rather than face it all head on.

In my own situation, if we continued living to the same standard as before, it wouldn't have been long before we crashed and burned in our finances. I'm not saying it wasn't a struggle, filled with uneven spending patterns and friction.

Sometimes, one partner has no past experience of cutting back and it will take a long time to rectify his or her poor money habits. He/she will justify all expenses as "reward for hard work" or "needed to relax". In this case, try to remember, "I am responsible for my own actions... I can choose to reduce spending where the end result is not a deal breaker".

The emotional stress of a personal crisis can also make people act out of character, for example, he or she:

- Continues living the same lifestyle but off lines of credit (head in the sand approach)
- Is gambling their only cash away, hoping for a windfall.
- Gets into a rage regularly

- Is highly defensive/argumentative (and this is not usual)
- Has panic attacks (and this is not usual)

Other symptoms of stress include:

- Headaches
- Anxiety
- Fatigue
- Heart palpitations
- Insomnia
- Overeating or other eating disorders
- Mood swings
- Poor concentration
- Stomach upsets
- Neck and back aches
- Dental problems from grinding teeth
- Depression
- Binge drinking
- Sexual arousal problems

If you are identifying with some of the above, this means that you could be having a reaction to your situation. To ease your suffering, you and your partner, if you have one, could seek the help of an understanding counsellor and doctor. Empathetic friends can also help your state of mind.

The understandable domestic conflicts and emotional fallout from money worries can bring a loving couple to the brink of separation. And if neither seeks counselling nor attempts some reflection and meaningful conversations, it's likelier that the ongoing conflict will end in divorce.

Often each will try to lay the blame or put the stress on the other. This is putting salt on the wound. Stone-walling is another communication blocker (a hurtful silence, the cold shoulder). This can lead to the other person feeling ignored and very unimportant.

If you want to keep your best friend and lover through a crisis, then it's time to change how you handle everyday communication.

TAKING RESPONSIBILITY AND LISTENING

Instead of blaming and directing what the other person should or shouldn't do, which is pointless, try to focus on your own feelings and behaviour.

Active listening is paramount. I learnt to listen and reflect, thanks to a financial counselling course. Reflecting means summarising what your partner has just said, or re-wording it to how you understand those feelings and asking "does that sound right?"

Learning to really listen to my partner, and identify and reflect his feelings, had two benefits. First, I found out what his overall feelings and worries were, engendering more empathy from me, and second, he felt more listened to and able to think of reasonable solutions. Often men speak plainly and logically, leaving their feelings unsaid. In reality their feelings are still there, but you'll need to have all your senses turned on to uncover what they are!

The polar opposite, women tend to react or explode with a torrent of their feelings in an argument. When it's your turn, frame what you say in terms of "I feel" or "I believe", but leave out the bit where you might normally say "you should" or "you never".

First try to understand what is the root cause of your partner's angst and empathise with that, for example, "Well anyone would feel that way" or, "I can understand that". This acknowledges their feelings.If the blame is coming from them with vitriol, then take time out for a while and say nothing right then.

Using these techniques can reduce the escalation your arguments. Active listening can have a profound effect on your relationship. It stops you from focusing on 'being right', which is a highway to nowhere. It pays to remember this:

Seek first to understand, then to be understood

(Habit #5 by Stephen Covey, '7 Habits of Highly-Effective People')

It's easy to get into fights with your partner when you're lacking in money. One partner may keep overspending beyond the income and simply will not cut back... but why?

I delved deep to try to understand my own spouse's overly defensive reactions to my suggestions of cost cutting (rather than make more money, as was his focus). Years afterward, I asked him how he felt then, in a totally non-threatening, interested way. His reflections were:

"Didn't want to go backwards".

"Frustration at the situation" (working long hours but not getting results)

"Felt like I was being attacked".

These types of reasons are what is known as "the root of the argument". I wished I had known this at the time, as it would have been much easier to be supportive. So look out for indications of what the root of the argument and underlying feelings really are, and then try to come to some sort of mutual understanding.

OTHER FEELINGS HOLDING YOU POWERLESS

Another money crisis emotion is *shame*. In my voluntary work, I often encountered people clearly feeling shame—particularly so with past overspending or having to leave a partner. Feeling shame over not being able to get a job… or guilt at the tussle between motherhood and earning an income… it's all debilitating until you can name it and explore it together with someone kind.

Pride can be useful or not useful; my partner felt too proud to accept the end of a business but eventually came around to a new solution. Pride is dandy when you are managing fine.

If you are feeling too proud, remember that church charities and Government benefits were set up to help people that need it when they need it; for you, this may be for just 2 or 3 months, and you may never need it again.

Often when a person is in the pain of crisis—with no real solutions—a lot of energy is spent deflecting that pain. Unhelpful remedies include binge drinking, taking unhealthy pills, shouting, gambling, infidelity, etc.

The first most powerful thing for anyone in crisis is to be truly listened to. (Listen to each other, as a start). Being listened to is one of those vital human needs. Think how many personal problems and workplace relations could be healed with much better listening.

The second most powerful thing is to be still and listen to your inner knowing. Try an audio guided meditation or a class if you're not familiar with meditating.

GETTING HELP

When you're suffering from a job loss or business cash flow crisis, the absolute worst thing you can do is try to ignore it or wait. Acting quickly to get some help will lessen not only the practical fallout, but it can also prevent feelings of helplessness and depression in some people.

For problems in a relationship, a relationship counsellor will be able to work through the issues in the couple's life and background without any children hearing an argument. Kids can also be invited to talk about how they feel about it all in part of a session, if that seems appropriate. (You will often get a straight up comment from your child that will strike right at the problem).

Try not to feel ashamed of keeping your family well by accepting a free food parcel, furniture or a friend's hospitality. One day you too can help other people in a similar circumstance.

When you are in financial hardship, it is essential to contact everyone you owe money to. Ask if you can negotiate reduced payment arrangements while you are in financial difficulty, or a repayment holiday. This is called a 'hardship variation'. As long as you have contacted utilities or lenders and are working with them to make payments, you should not be hassled by debt collectors at this stage… although well overdue unpaid debts may still go on your credit record.

I recommend you seek a free financial counsellor/debt counselor. You'll find contact numbers in the Resources section. Also find your local Neighborhood Centre and ask for what resources you most need (they can't pay your bills but it's amazing what can be sought or referred).

Act as If

At a different time in my life, upon leaving a spouse, it was a case of having to act together and happy in order to secure a job and a place to live. With two weeks in which to get employment and no social security safety net, I secured a job interview and tried the "act as if" technique (thanks to Tony Robbins' 'Get the Edge' program for this concept).

The "act as if" strategy is: smiling, walking tall, and shaking hands confidently. It fools your body into the best kind of body language. Smiling actually makes one feel happier. Your body then fools your mind that everything is perfectly fine (for a time), you talk excitedly, envisioning success, and with a bit of practice, you get what you want.

I got my job in marketing and I paid my first month's rent.

DEPRESSION

"What few people realise is that thought and feeling are connected in a two-way loop."[3] - Sam Cawthorn

This loop means that if you keep thinking, "I'm down", "nothing goes right for me", then you'll start to feel the hallmarks of depression: misery, lethargy, short fuse, etc.

After three decades of research, a professor named Martin E.P. Seligman, found that pessimists are more prone to feel helpless, and prolonged helplessness can cause the symptoms known as depression. Maybe this is why folk visiting Neighbourhood Centre emergency relief seemed to me to show depressive symptoms (crying, tired, angry, irritable).

Seligman's book 'Learned Optimism' carries much insight into the role of optimism, and why we all need it so badly. Pessimism is rife among those in the lower socio-economic strata, along with external blame of misfortune.

17

But then again, those with a pessimistic streak may also have regular periods where things go just fine.

If you find yourself tired, an insomniac, stressed and shaky over the period of your crisis, this is a response to your situation. If you tell your Doctor about the symptoms and she or he begins to prescribe you an antidepressant (likely an SSRI), question why you need this without at least a test or referral for psychological help.

When you present with sadness, inability to sleep, and perhaps heart palpitations and panic attacks, why does the doc often reach for dangerous antidepressants without a proper test or waiting to see if your situation is going to be short-lived? The answer is two-fold.

Depression has been widely classed as an ongoing mental illness, and it seems anyone with a combination of these typical problems can be called 'depressed'. Labels like this only serve to victimise people under stress, particularly when they are faced with the authority of a man or woman in a white coat.

Typical symptoms are often the effects of stressors that have overloaded the person. Crying and feeling angry may even stem from old neural pathways that almost get 'stuck in one rut' as the person ruminates on the negative. Yet it does not have to be a permanent condition.

The second reason that contributes to the number of antidepressant prescriptions is the fact that doctors are often swayed into prescribing them by the claptrap information that pharmaceutical companies provide. Huge profits are at stake.

While it is often said that it's better to prevent a possible suicide by offering these so-called 'safe' drugs, in certain cases when an antipsychotic or antidepressant drug is given to otherwise normal people, this can actually perpetuate a suicide. Rebekah Beddoe's harrowing personal tale *'Dying for a Cure'* explains how she went from having post-natal downs to getting over-medicated on four drugs, as the first one propelled her to harm and suicidal ideas. Her story contradicts the notion of safe antidepressant drugs that are easy to withdraw from.[5]

Another author, Soraya Saraswati, tells her account of her son's suicide after being given an antipsychotic medication (while in hospital) in her book, *'Shining Through: From Grief to Gratitude'.*[6]

It is still up in the air how many of those receiving antidepressants are actually helped by them. Prozac (for 25 years it was prescribed for any kind of depression) started its life as a heart medication. Later trials showed some regularly happy people felt suicidal/depressed on the drug. Hello common sense?

Prior to the 1990s, people with clinical depression existed of course, as they do now, but drugs (with known side effects) were given more judiciously. In fact, it has never been proven that those suffering depressive symptoms have a 'chemical imbalance' i.e. a lack of balance in serotonin levels, which are what SSRIs are designed to correct.

We all have a mix of brain chemicals and hormones that can affect mood, so to pin down just one seems impossible, when you think about it.

Even *The Journal of the American Medical Association* (a highly respected journal) reported that "anti-depressants were no more effective in treating mild to moderate depression than a placebo."[7]

Simpler Solutions

Luckily, there are other ways to ease depressive feelings and tension. According to a little-known theory, it is the forming of new neural pathways (the new connections between brain cells) that can ultimately free people from the ongoing feelings of depression[8].

To benefit from this 'rewire-able brain', the depressed person must participate in new activities daily, activities that stimulate grey matter growth and create new neural pathways. One way to do this is to get regular exercise that moves the body in new ways.[8]

> Pessimism and hopelessness seem to block prosperity, while optimistic thinking will help anyone bounce back from life's hardballs.

Since adapting to life changes of any kind is stressful, learning how to relax body and mind can be helpful. Joining in with yoga, tai chi, or meditation class, listening to relaxing music or guided meditation, going for a walk along the beach, or learning breathing techniques for relaxation are just some ways you can use to cope with stress… and restore inner harmony and balance.

Music therapy is an alternative that may be useful for reducing stress and anxiety amid life changes. Music is good for the soul, and it has been around since time immemorial.

Exercising to a 'near puffing' level releases endorphins and is also a known stress reliever. It sounds simplistic, but regular exercise, a nutritious diet, quality sleep and relaxation… while limiting stimulants (like alcohol, coffee and energy drinks) and excess sugars… means that usually you'll become energised naturally. So you'll be more able to cope with any kind of stress. (Caffeine can over-stimulate the adrenal glands and make depression worse).

Nutrition. Did you know that much of our vegetables and fruit these days don't have all the nutrients they once did? Supermarket supplied fruit like grapes, apples and strawberries also carry toxins from pesticide spray. So, unless you eat an all-organic cup of vegetables and pick a fresh unsprayed apple every day, you may need a good quality vitamin and mineral supplement to get the energy for life.

If you want to make your own remedies, try green 'superfood' powder to liquid drinks… or make your own fresh juices with fresh kale, spinach leaves, cucumber, celery or carrot, adding pineapple, mango, banana, apple and/or pear for natural sweetness. If you do add the greens and water to your juice, be prepared for a bouncy energy and a feeling of fullness.

Herbs for Relieving Depression:

- St John's Wort
- Lemon balm
- Hawthorn

If you are able to see a herbalist or holistic doctor first, please do so to make sure these herbs are right for you. Take by mixing the herbs and pouring boiling water over them, 1 cup of water per 1 Tablespoon herb, and steep for 60 minutes or longer. Then enjoy this tea 3-4 times a day. Use a strainer.[12]

If you can't find these herbs, there are herbal supplements in tablet form that need to be prescribed by a doctor/naturopath.

What about diet? People suffering depression are often found to be lacking in essential fatty acids. You can get this by eating oily fish or taking fish oil, flaxseed oil or evening primrose oil every day. Recommended total amount for adults is 1500 mg daily [12], but see your natural therapist for advice.

INSPIRATION AND RELAXATION

For inspiration to move past crisis, try listening to audiobooks or reading ebooks like: *The Success Principles, The Seven Habits of Highly-Effective People, Daring Greatly, Our Erroneous Zones,* and more.

Connecting with the universal laws and hearing inspiring people's stories gives you hope... the elixir of life. Not only that, it helps to better understand yourself and your relationships.

Learning the art of deep tissue massage could also benefit a couple or two friends. It's said that massage may release not just tension, but also deep-seated emotions and sad memories. A drop of lavender essential oil in the carrier oil can be very relaxing.

Another low-cost therapy that relaxes and relieves stress is bathing with rose petals, real lavender/lavender oil, and oats.[12]

Now, before exploring how to go about our 'practical' recovery, let's delve into an often-overlooked catalyst of business or personal failures—our beliefs and values.

Chapter 2

Beliefs and Values

Intelligence and education has nothing to do with finding and keeping wealth. For example, I've read lots of books about investing and success, I have a degree, and I've accrued many skills. None of this helped much when a personal income crisis hit us... although it helped to have a little faith.

The reason for our financial insecurity was down to our strong beliefs and values, and each individual's focus.

My spouse's belief was: "creating websites for small business is fulfilling creatively, but it will never make us enough money". And so it was to be.

My belief was: "if I just focus on cutting costs, supporting my partner's business, looking after my daughter, and performing my writing service with leftover time, that is all I can do".

While I put the making money thing as last priority, I did very well on the cost cutting! I put what I learned into a short book, *How to Kick Bad Spending Habits.*

A belief is nothing more than a generalization about the world or your ability, which then determines what behaviours and actions you allow yourself to experience.

- Christopher Howard *(From Passion to Profit, 2012)*

Beliefs about our personal limits can be wrong, dead wrong. Usually we see this in hindsight, after we have achieved, quite surprisingly, more than we thought we could.

This poem from the book *Think and Grow Rich* is about how it takes no more effort to aim high (for prosperity and abundance) than is needed to aim low, accepting misery and poverty.

"I bargained with Life for a penny,

And Life would pay no more,

However I begged at evening

When I counted my scanty score.

For Life is a just employer,

He gives you what you ask,

But once you have set the wages,

Why, you must bear the task.

I worked for a menial's hire,

Only to learn, dismayed,

That any wage I had asked of Life,

Life would have willingly paid."

Obviously this poet went on from earning peanuts to a better life, through the tough route of experience! Can you relate to that?

Beliefs Stem from Values

Beliefs stem from values. As our values are strongly family (our daughter first), this shared value affected all our decisions. You might find the same.

A shift for both of us to regular full-time jobs would have had a big impact on our daughter, who was parentally attached and sensitive. Therefore we did not view it as a good option, in fact, love portrayed itself as stubborn refusal (and I'm not saying that it's good or bad).

You can see below where a value relates to a belief.

Prime Value	Corresponding belief (example)
Work/Caretaking	To be a good caretaker, I must work very hard to be a success even if that means not being there
Family	To be a good Mum, I must look after my kids full time, or bend over backwards for them
Career	I need to focus on my job and not have children, because that would mean loss of career track and loss of pay

Relationship	My partners' outlook controls my money life; I can't do anything while he/she is spending
Pleasure	The retail therapy I get from shopping is more important than the fact I'm in debt

Some of these beliefs are an example of 'polarised' thinking – not seeing the grey areas/options in between. For the person owning them, her perceptions are her reality. But are they a reality that serves in the long run?

Beliefs are pre-programmed and therefore difficult to change—even if your life would be better if they did! To make enduring change, you need to access your unconscious and clear those limits away. Tools to do this include: deep meditation, kinesiology, and to some extent, NLP (neuro-linguistic programming) or CBT (Cognitive Behavioural Therapy). A trained practitioner can help you out in one of these areas.

MONEY AS A BELIEF

Your beliefs about money may have come straight from your parents or been influenced by peers (not necessarily happy and successful ones). Has a parent ever said, "Money is not important", or "We don't talk finances at the dinner table"? If so, think about how this has influenced your life; perhaps you have never learned about investing or you unthinkingly push any money issues aside whenever it comes up (in your preprogram, it's not important).

Or maybe you thought being lousy at math meant you would be lousy at personal finances, as it involved numbers too. (Thanks to online calculators and budgeting software, you don't even have to use math skills to figure your finances out). The basic tenet to know is:

Money in must equal or be more than *money out*.

While other things are important, trying to live in today's world without any valued medium of exchange is nigh on impossible—unless you enjoy living in tents and eating beans. So can we agree that money is important—and knowledge of how to grow your money would really help?

What other confining beliefs do professional adults commonly have?

- That they must put in 45 to 80 hours a week at work and be continually connected, in order to succeed

- That their income must relate to a certain dollar figure per hour (usually the same as their peers), OR

- That their small business/self-employment monetary success is entirely reflective of how good they are at their specialty, not what they can learn and apply in other crucial areas

- That they cannot earn a bountiful income doing what they enjoy and for the greater good.

Can you see how these kinds of beliefs confine your decisions and limit your prosperity and joy in life? Limiting beliefs often stop us from trying new things, such as starting a new home business, or investing in shares, or studying part-time in a field we believe we would enjoy.

Many of your current decisions and thoughts regarding money may stem from your 'cognitive distortions', or in layman's terms, your limiting and erroneous beliefs. Our outlook, generally pessimistic or generally optimistic, seems to determine many of our repetitive thoughts.

Now what would you rather be: mainly optimistic and attracting more prosperity and opportunity, or mainly pessimistic and repelling opportunity (and therefore, prosperity)?

Why not step back and observe the pessimistic or optimistic framing that takes place in your mind or your speech. If you tend to identify with the left of the table, then look at how to reframe these common thoughts and take more responsibility for your life:

RE-FRAMING THOUGHTS

NEGATIVE FRAMING	POSITIVE FRAMING
I've never got enough	I've got more than enough
That business is booming – I bet they're all crooks	Look at how well X is doing, they must have a sound business. Maybe I can read their story.

I can never seem to get ahead (frustration)	I am going to learn various ways to save money and leverage what I get, to get ahead
I could start my own business if I just had the funds	I can access the funds I need by looking on the Internet for grants and even crowdfund if I have an excellent idea.
If my partner/parent had been more supportive, I'd be a success right now.	I can only start from where I am now. I choose to just get started in my dream field, even if it's low down the tree or working part-time for someone else. It was my choice before to listen to others, but now I choose to learn and earn in any way that fits in with my commitments.
You can't get ahead on my lousy pay-cheque	I choose to allocate at least 5% of income to savings and build up to 10%, because I work hard and deserve to get ahead.

It's important to re-frame your thoughts with a more powerful "I" statement. This is because you are now taking responsibility for what happens in your life. Only you can decide to stop blaming other things for a lack of action and progress, and only you can quit complaining.

Another reason is because the words we speak and think need to align with what we want to do and achieve. If they clash, then there will be no moving forward. This is a tenet proven by the experience of Maha Sinnathamby, the co-creator of Greater Springfield master planned community, who was once a broke immigrant student. One of Maha's idols was Mahatma Ghandi, who also believed that truth must be applied in all our words and actions, so that all our deeds are aligned to the moral code, the universal truth of God.

(You can read about Maha's ten principles in his book *"Stop Not Till Your Goal is Reached"*).

Our digital age is certainly the age of the entrepreneur who starts from nothing and builds a company in a lean way. But this does take business knowhow, connections, and concerted effort.

There are also easy-to-start opportunities to earn money by commission selling, or by starting a service, or by selling information online. The Australian government helps those who are Centrelink benefit recipients to start a business, with a NEIS income support for 39 weeks and mentoring too. Other startup programs, grants and training support are also available for the serious few. See **www.business.gov.au/assistance**.

So you see, re-framing your thoughts opens your eyes to the many possibilities that exist around you.

CHANGING BELIEFS TO HELP YOU GROW AND INVEST

Christopher Howard (an authority on personal influence and NLP) believes it is possible to change your mind's thought processes and behaviour through education. It's often the very people who need to change their beliefs the most who shy away from self-education or coaching. So I congratulate you for having an open mind.

Overall, we don't want to let outdated beliefs rule our decisions.

Slow-footedness to develop your career or grow an ideal business is likely to stem from a lack of self-belief and imposed limitations. But at least if you are aware of this, you can take small steps towards that goal, thus proving (to yourself) that you could have a different future. For example, you can contact someone already doing the role of your heart's desire, and discuss what is good and bad about it.

Even when contemplating investing, limiting beliefs stand in our way. Maybe you think, "I don't know how to invest so I'll ask a financial advisor or attend that free property seminar". So you go along and they sell you on the outcomes you want. In this sales environment, they will most often appeal to your greed, and possibly to your fear of retiring in poverty. You might forget that it's completely up to you to make it happen.

You may also be operating from the false belief that you aren't smart enough to learn about investing wisely (which you are) and forgetting that intuition will guide you to the right path (which it will, if you listen). But never listen to that greedy or fearful inner voice, because as you can observe from the many booms and busts that come in cycles, greed and fear has got many an everyday investor into hot water.

You also must enjoy this process of investing, whatever path you think is 'me'. That's right — love the way you invest and enjoy what you invest in.

Instead of running around looking for answers from all these 'experts' who want to sell to you, take the time to ask, "am I going to be happy rushing to the screen every day to look at positions in the market, and am I mentally fit to handle when the market goes against my position?"

VALUE-BASED DECISIONS

Life comes so much easier when you base decisions on your values, instead of on money or on obligation.

That said, some people cannot seem to earn very much (or make good investments) as they strongly identify as 'carers'. They might carry an unconscious belief that carers cannot also earn much money. It's a conflicting position based on years of unconscious judgments, not the truth.

If you happen to identify as a carer, look for role models who care for the world and also attract abundance. You will find people who give back to the community as much as or more than they keep themselves; that's what feels right for them. Philanthropic entrepreneurs who fundraise for children, Aid field workers who give as doctors and nurses, kind landladies—these people come from all walks of life and offer all kinds of care.

You can start looking via any Facebook connections you have and also wander the aisles of the crowdfunding sites.

33

Let's Check Your Highest Values

If you ponder all your values and keep them in mind, it will be easier to just say 'no' to unwanted demands, or to delegate low-value activities. For instance, get a mower service so you can spend Sundays with your family instead of the lawn.

So, examine now your satisfaction with each life zone, and give each area a score out of 10:

Family

Intimate relationship

Health & Body zone

Spiritual / self zone

Contribution / community zone

Money zone

Career / business zone

This will help you realise which areas need some more attention. If your spouse seems unhappy with what time you give them, this indicates that this relationship needs more quality attention from you. If your body looks untoned, out of proportion and you feel lethargic, then it must be your health & body that needs some TLC.

A balanced life really means that we feel comfortably balanced across these zones, although the time spent in each may not be even.

Supreme focus on earning more all the time means that your life might well be full of regrets and stress. Because of money worries, you might be suffering from the 'work harder' syndrome. You work harder and harder, but feel less and less fulfilled and respected. This resentment build-up will never bring you peace and money.

So, making time for inner work on your self is essential. Two primary things to work on are: forgiveness (others and yourself) and gratitude. This is daily work, not just a one off thing.

Listening to others, to their core needs and feelings (rather than the froth on top) is likewise essential for relationships.

With this in place, I think you'll find that relationships, love and money will flow more easily.

So go ahead and schedule some more weekly time in for your most important areas. I encourage you every night at 8 o'clock or so to switch off phones, switch off the TV, and tune into what you really want and value.

CHAPTER 3

SUCCESS PRINCIPLES FROM THOUGHT

Can you guess the #1 thing that's probably stopping you from enjoying prosperity? It has been written about throughout the years, over and over again. Just look at the titles of top personal growth bestsellers:

Think and Grow Rich – by Napoleon Hill
Secrets of the Millionaire Mind – T. Harv Eker
The Power of Intention – Wayne Dwyer

All these books talk about the power of your thoughts and intention.So, the first key to unlock your future good fortune and success is to change your mindset.

Most people need a lot of help to retrain their thinking. It's taken a lifetime of bad clichés and poor ideas from others to build the wall, and it's going to take sheer determination to knock that sucker down. Think of all the times you've heard from parents, or said yourself:

"We just can't afford it"

"Money doesn't grow on trees"

"Money can't buy happiness"

"There's never enough money to pay the bills"

"They're filthy rich" "The rich are greedy crooks, etc"

"Money is the source of all evil"

"I don't need money"

Your past programming is no doubt still running through your mind. Some call it "self-talk". There may be a whole lot of negative self-talk influencing your whole life. You may also carry barely-recognised doubts and misconceptions that are stopping you from stepping forward.

"No thought lives in your head rent-free"

- Robert Allen, author

This saying is about how you pay for negative thoughts. You really pay for negativity... in income, in energy, in health and how happy you are. A negative mindset is cancerous... but why?

"What You Focus On... Expands"

I keep this phrase imprinted on my brain... so every time a negative thought pops into my head, like "we can't pay all these bills, it's just so much", my reminding voice says, "are you crazy? Do you want your bills and money problems to expand? Let's focus on the positives".

> People who have the power of intention never talk about their problems now, as that would just attract more of it, they talk about what they INTEND to achieve. (Paraphrased).
>
> – Wayne Dyer, Secrets of the Power of Intention.

Wayne Dyer's teachings always remind me how to put the attention on what I want, not what I don't want. Many walks I've had around the park, listening to *Secrets of the Power of Intention* (an audiobook). At a crucial time, this helped me have faith and focus on what I want.

Every time I use the power of intention… just putting it out there and going forth with gusto… the right people or opportunities seem to show up in my life. But whenever I give up on my dreams and settle for less, that's exactly what I get. Less.

Going through hard financial times pushed me to read more about positive psychology and changing mental habits. I encourage you to find out more about this too. Observe what works best for you.

(Further reading: *'Rewire your Brain'* by John B Arden, or *'The Brain that Changes Itself'* by Norman Doidge, MD).

What's Your Inner Motivation?

If you are currently motivated by money in this way:

"I work just to pay the bills", or

"I don't want to be broke"

Then you are operating from a pain-motivated perspective. Your unconscious mind attaches itself to the real focus, "paying bills" or "being broke". Unfortunately, you're unlikely to move beyond a fragile financial state with these current thoughts. But through self-awareness, you can change this focus… and your results.

We're really talking about changing from pessimistic to optimistic thinking.

Once you change from a pain-motivated perspective to a positive, future perspective, a strange thing will happen. Say you write a goal down, with the most self-motivating reason written beside it. You're fired up for this goal but not desperately seeking answers. While you're not even thinking about your goals, say you're relaxing or showering, your mind will come up with a good idea (a eureka!) to bring you closer to your exciting goal.

When your subconscious mind gives you a great idea, what do you usually do with it? Do you consider your subconscious, which tirelessly works on tricky problems you have, to be a nuisance? Or do you rush off, note it in your notebook and get straight into investigating the possibility of it?

A little known book called "Talk and Grow Rich" taught me to still the mind and listen out for an inner 'eureka'. It's your subconscious giving you the very solutions you've asked for, which happens after setting goals. Occasionally a solution comes up unexpectedly in a more concrete fashion, but often the best ones just spring from your mind. Amazing, eh?

I was always looking everywhere else for success, and there it was all along, right under my nose.

HAPPINESS AND SUCCESS – IS IT POSSIBLE?

Have you seen primary kids get out of school, running and jumping, happy just to be alive? When my daughter talks about learning music, her face lights up. Why don't adults run, skip, and smile when they come out of their workplace? You see them in the city, heads down, wearing somber colors and even more somber expressions.

What do you think happens when we become an adult? We are taught to conform, confine our beliefs, and not to follow our passions. Have a 'eureka!' idea and people may say, "that's a pipe-dream", or "you can't live on dreams". But the most depressing thought of all, to me, is to not be able to dream of our own big, exciting future.

Plus, how true is that big dreams don't bring big success? Because when Napoleon Hill researched 504 of the world's wealthiest people, the opposite seems to have been proven true, in many different anecdotes.[10] His book 'Think and Grow Rich' (1937) became a long-lived bestseller.

In *Think and Grow Rich*, Mr. Hill narrates an idea for cheaper steel and a united trust, started in the mind of Charles M Schwab and conveyed in an impassioned speech to 80 of the richest men in America. Many had tried to convince magnates J.P. Morgan and Andrew Carnegie to join forces before but failed. The result of Mr. Schwab's strong vision was the United States Steel

Corporation, a billion-dollar enterprise.

In his studies over 25 years, Mr. Hill found 13 essential principles for creating wealth and success. The book starts with the most important one, the one he refers to as 'the secret hidden in this book':

1. A burning desire to attain a goal

2. Faith

3. Auto-suggestion (or controlling what is sensed and thought by you)

4. Organized planning and strong leadership

5. Applying specialized knowledge

6. Imagination and ideas

7. Decision – the opposite of procrastination

8. Persistence (and tying it to your dire need)

9. The Mastermind group – i.e. an organized team working towards a common goal.

10. Harnessing the power of sexual desire and directing it to creative endeavor.

11. Planting desires in the subconscious mind.

12. Using the power of the brain

13. The sixth sense.

Not only do big dreams and persistence backed by "a burning desire" work better than thinking small, big dreams have enabled great inventions, enterprises, and charitable works for centuries. The greatest of inventions have come from minds not bounded by other people's fears, doubts and misconceptions.

Of all the success factors listed above, when starting to claw our way back from financial mess, the attributes that helped me the most were: having faith, making a public commitment, and focusing on a positive future in my mind.[11 & 12]

By commitment, I mean a firm choice to follow my dreams and aims, rather than fall prey to excuses and alibis.

Through our faith comes a sense of peace, and through our positive future vision (also written as goals) comes a sense of power.

BECOMING MORE RESILIENT

Many psychologists believe that people can learn how to become more resilient and happier. Founder of the modern Positive Psychology movement around 25 years ago, Martin Seligman believes that we can create our own happiness. His methods include Learned Optimism and Learned Resourcefulness.

Seligman's early studies included animal trials on helplessness as well as an analysis on all kinds of people's explanations of events, which he then used to tell if they tended to be optimistic. He also applied this test to tell if winning sports teams were made up of optimistic explainers—they were.

Why not use an hour to measure some aspects of your

authentic happiness and identify your best strengths (for free) at: **www.authentichappiness.org**

Find Martin Seligman's TED talk to better understand positive psychology: **www.ted.com.**

We need resilience and a positive outlook if we are ever going to be financially successful and quickly get back on our feet after difficulties. Yet we all have different abilities to cope. If no-one has ever taught you any skills in becoming more positive, you could be forgiven for thinking, when disaster strikes, that a) the world is against you, and b) you have no control.

I believe you can choose to change your life—so that it's not all just paying bills, grinding obligations, and shitty bosses (or no work at all). It's really up to you to make brave choices.

Ten Concepts to Get You Through a Rough Patch

1. Making decisions based on your core values, rather than money alone, leads to better outcomes overall.

2. If you commit to your goals, any hardship seems 'character-building' rather than just hard.

3. The bigger the sacrifice, the greater the reward. (Just don't sacrifice all your time for wages).

4. Living off of credit—dumb. Scaling back lifestyle to suit—smart.

43

5. Creating beautiful things is good for the soul... and often leads to a new venture.

6. Sell things that you've no need for anymore, to declutter your space and attract the new.

7. Tell other parents, friends, neighbours, etc that you're looking for an extra job, or better clients, and explain your value.

8. If this crisis is caused by a spouse, then divide your finances, get your own accounts and run a budget that's fair (i.e. not leaving out a dependant).

9. Share your troubles with a financial counsellor or family support worker, thus getting help to find resources and cheap/free food and furniture.

10. Stop comparing yourself to others of your age. Start preparing yourself for the next 10 exciting years.

GET INTO THE RIGHT FLOW

Here is a gem in *Think and Grow Rich*, where Mr. Hill talks about the "stream of power". On one side, the stream flows onwards and upwards, taking those in its flow to wealth, and on the other side it flows the opposite way, carrying all that have the misfortune to get into its flow, downward to misery:

> "The positive emotions of thought form the side of the stream which carries one to fortune. The negative emotions form the side which carries one down to poverty."

If you're like many people, you probably flick from positive thoughts to negative, or else stay in the negative. After a while I came to recognise the total negativity when a debt relief client talked about their bills, even though they may only have said a few words.

It seems that these ordinary people just didn't want to know about their own financial affairs. Some people alluded to the fact that they never had much of a handle on money, while others said, "I don't know how much I spend on average on groceries". And yet they do it over and over again, so their avoidance techniques are very good!

So why do they avoid it all?

Perhaps because they now see their whole money zone as negative: too many bills are negative, results from reliance on credit cards are negative, debt brought the business down... need I go on?

With negative thought habits and emotions in your money zone, you would continue to experience money troubles forever... if you did nothing different. I have lived it, it's no fun, and the only way out is to become more aware and control your thoughts. Controlling your thoughts and planning your actions leads to better and more positive results.

So what could be the catalyst to change those very confining thoughts? Perhaps it's when your last straw has broke, perhaps you've tried numerous ways to get a job and you're simply feeling defeated... but you now have a powerful reason to apply concerted effort in order to reach your goal. Part of this effort could be trying cognitive therapy techniques or positive thinking/positive psychology.

So what is Cognitive Behavioural Therapy?

CBT variations are often used in treating disorders of the mind, including depression. It teaches patients to identify and challenge negative thought patterns and errors in beliefs. For depression, patients are often asked to write down their thoughts after something unsettling happens, then these thoughts are discussed with the trained therapist. Are they accurate and useful?

We need neuroplasticity (the brain's elastic ability to alter its structure, to 'rewire' itself) to work properly to help us recover from trauma and negative thoughts. CBT has been shown to encourage more positive thinking and build new neural pathways in those with minor depression. Although, a new study has shown that in people with longstanding major depression, this rewiring process is impaired.[7]

Repeating positive statements to yourself usually helps you feel better... and sharing positivity could even rewire your brain to be more optimistic.

Benefits of Positive Thinking

Far from being a hippy-dippy idea, positive thinking and attitude has far-reaching health and other life benefits. And when you have problems in life, with a positive mindset you can attack those challenges more productively.

It Helps You Avoid Depression

Pessimistic thinking is one of the factors in depression. Just changing negative self-talk into more positive self-talk causes a positive mental mood that helps combat depression. This is why Cognitive Therapy – changing patterns of thought to help improve mood – is now widespread in treating depression.

It Can Help You Secure a Job

A 2008 study of recently unemployed people by the Georgia Institute of Technology for five months (or until they landed a new job) found that those people who stayed positive and were persistent in their search found work sooner. During this time, those who had developed routines, sought support, and kept defeatist thoughts at bay, were also those who put in the most hours on their search. By end of the study, 72 percent had found new jobs.[9]

It Can Help You Recover from Cancer or Heart Disease

It was found that people with positive attitudes recover faster from surgery and cope better with serious diseases, such as cancer, heart disease and AIDS (study by Psych Central, mental health professional network).

University of Pittsburgh (School of Medicine) studied 100,000 postmenopausal women and found that those who were optimistic were 30% less likely to die from heart disease than pessimists, while the negative thinkers were 23% more likely to die from cancer. [Crikey! Let's not die from negative thoughts!]

You Model Positive Thinking for your Child

A recent study even found that children as young as five know the benefits of positive thinking. Most kids predicted that people would feel better after thinking positive thoughts, than they would after thinking negative thoughts.

"The strongest predictor of children's knowledge about the benefits of positive thinking—besides age—was not the child's own level of hope and optimism, but their parents," said study leader Christi Bamford, Ph.D.[11]

So we all have a role to play in modeling a positive outlook on events for our child, whether it's a broken cup or missing out on a part in the school play. A positive spin by the parent will help the child learn to think positively.

Self-Help

Sometimes self-awareness is enough. Simply journaling your thoughts over a period of time could help. (Look back and see the patterns in thinking).

As a past negative thinker, I found that changes in my negativity occurred after 3-4 hours a week of inspiring messages in the form of self-help audio books, podcasts, videos, or books. (It really doesn't matter the form, it's the positive content and inspiring stories that you need). Perhaps you have some positive friends to talk to, which also helps greatly, so don't freak out about the time!

Try this technique:

Put on your wrist a rubber band. For one week, every time you think a negative thought or say a limiting comment or a justification for failing, flip that sucker. Your wrist may get sore but you will re-train your mind for positive thinking. (Idea courtesy of 'One Minute Millionaire' by Mark V Hansen and Robert G Allen).

Postscript: Positive mental attitude is not just a nice idea; the right thoughts and beliefs are the fuel that will help propel you onwards to success.

Now you know that it's crucial to get your emotional mind in order before getting your finances in order. I know you're eager to get to the practical budgeting stuff, but first there is something really big and important to do…

Chapter 4

Setting Big Goals

"Tenacity is setting a goal so BIG you can't possibly achieve it...then growing into the person who can"

– Tamara McCleary

So Why Write Goals Down?

While there has been much said by gurus about studies of graduates who wrote their goals down, these are urban legends. That said, writing your goals is a proven wise step. A small study at the Dominican University of 149 business people from varied backgrounds reinforced that goal writing and accountability principles were more effective than carrying a goal in your head. The conclusions of the study were:

1. The positive effect of accountability was supported: those who sent weekly progress reports to their friend accomplished significantly more than those who had unwritten goals, or even those who wrote their goals or formulated action commitments.

2. There was support for the role of public commitment: those who sent their commitments to a friend accomplished significantly more than those who wrote action commitments or did not write their goals.

3. The positive effect of written goals was supported: those who wrote their goals accomplished significantly more than those who did not write their goals.

You can see it's powerful if you can share your goals with as many people as possible. Look what it did for Julie (of 'Julie and Julia'), who committed publicly to cook every recipe from Julia Child's French Cooking book, no matter how difficult it was. Sharing with even one friend invokes the psychological principle of being consistent (with what you say). Finally you can use this principle for your own good.

TAKE ACTION!

Another thing you must do is take immediate action on your goals. A set of big goals is only useful if you break them down into smaller, manageable steps that allow you to progress naturally towards them.

Many people try to shortcut their success or get over their fears by buying a guru's course. Having read many horror stories of this path, it is infinitely better to "choose your own path". Learn yourself, with the help of solid personal finance books/podcasts. For example, perhaps you like Scott Pape's Barefoot Investor teachings. Then apply those money philosophies of his you like to your own financial goals. It certainly helps to have a 'mojo' account, which I call my rainy day fund.

Be, Do, Have Goal Setting

Making goals for what you want to 'be, do and have' can give you powerful clarity. You may have heard of this if you have read Tim Ferris' book or blog (*The Four-Hour Work Week*).

It means: examples of what you want to be, stuff you want to do, and things you want to have. E.g. 'I want to be a fully qualified chef' is a 'being' goal.

Specific, measurable, achievable, results-focused and time-oriented (SMART) goals are important, as long as they are aligned to your personal values. So remember to write down your core values first.

Specific:

Write a goal that is full of colour; you can almost see it and feel it. Not just "I want a job", but "I want a job that is creative, fairly close to home, pays well, has a friendly working atmosphere, and allows for personal interaction".

Measurable:

Your goal must be easy to recognise once achieved. E.g. "once I complete my Bachelor degree, this goal is achieved."

ACHIEVABLE:

You can't go from barely puffing through a 3 kilometre run to doing a 40 kilometre marathon, but the next step of 10 kilometres within three months is achievable for this next stage.

RESULTS-FOCUSED:

Always state your outcomes, not simply what you'll do. For example, 'I aim to sell 1,000 books' (the final result), not just 'publishing a book and alerting friends and contacts'. These are results I can count, not the airy-fairy kind.

TIME-BOUND:

I am aiming to sell the 1,000 books by December 2016, after 10 different promotions. Giving a date to the goal sets it in your mind as a race to the finish line. As most of us know, goals without a deadline become lost and procrastinated wishes.

Remember to write your entire goal statement in your goals diary.

EXAMPLES

For now, here are some Big Goal examples:

Being a present and happy parent, with an hour a day for play / homework.

Being a profitable business operator with a $75,000 revenue stream by July 2017.

Doing: Going snorkeling with my family on the Great Barrier Reef by December 2017.

Having: Our first investment property by July 2018.

While you could go deeper, this type of goal setting is enough to motivate the socks off you, especially combined with a powerful visualization each day. We all have an imagination and a right to use it for inspiring ourselves to great things. (I found it motivates you better if you consider your goals deeply every day, but if this is not possible then try going deep into it every Sunday).

Take action now and get a Goals diary. The diary should be one that you are proud to write in and keep. Give those SMART goals a deadline that's not so tight it causes alarm... but not so far away that it lets you slack off.

After setting your goals and noting your values, make some time for a walk. As you walk, feel grateful for what you have already. Gratitude works like magic; the more you feel it, the better your life will become. (The opposite is also true).

If everything else is not so great, then be grateful for your surroundings or people in the past who were loving to you.

After this, visualise yourself and your family being present in the site of your dream goal.

Finally, forgive yourself for any past mistakes with money. Like any life event, in order to move on we must first forgive. But with money, forgiveness seems harder to do. Loss is hard, but equally, dying without achieving your dreams would be the worst loss of all. Blame and resentment is toxic, so also forgive significant others who have let you down or held you back.

Take a break now before reading "The Seven Pillars of Financial Sense".

PART TWO:

THE 7 PILLARS OF FINANCIAL SENSE

This is the 'hands on' action plan for your new life.

CHAPTER 5

PILLAR 1: BALANCING

Set up a Budget, so that all of your outgoings are less than your income.

Firstly, track your spending, either on paper, on your bank statement, or on a real-time budget planner like Pocketbook or Mint app.

After you have thought of all the different things that come up during the year, put those items and amounts into any pre-formed budget planner, along with inserting your total family income and assets/liabilities. If you do this in a spreadsheet, then asset values and liabilities would go on a different sheet. It's best to put in 12 months of projected costs and then budget monthly.

You want the ideal of more income than outgoings. When your budget is not balancing, you can either:

(1) increase your income, or (2) decrease your outgoings.

Debts you owe may be paid out of present and future income, but don't count on artificial income projections. Debt repayment must be realistic and broken down into manageable set amounts.

Last on the list is determining Holidays & Gifts budget and Car upgrade savings, as these are the most discretionary items.

What about loans for personal use? My belief is 'saving up' is a better way than lending and paying lots of interest. Think long term, not short term, remembering:

> The rich borrow to buy assets; the poor and middle-class borrow to buy lifestyle expenses!

My Budgeting Method

I use a Zero-Dollar Budgeting method, meaning every dollar earned is allocated an end purpose. Savings are also allocated.

One way to get through lean times is to smooth bills. The 'bill smoothing' concept is: every expenditure is broken down monthly, and every bill is paid towards monthly or allocated as savings towards it. (You can arrange this with some proactive Internet banking).

This smoothes your expenditure out, so that you are not tempted to overspend some months and then starve other months. You may also choose fortnightly, if that works better for your income flow.

SmoothPay is now offered by most utility suppliers.

ONLINE BUDGETING

You might be the kind of person who needs a mainly manual system that is easy to grasp. The CAP (Christians Against Poverty) money system or Envelope System is perfect for you. Myself, I prefer the type of system where I can allocate budget items and track real expenses, and still use the automated joys of online banking.

If you are an avid EFTPOS or Debit VISA˚ card user, it will be easier to use a system like Pocketbook or BudgetPulse. Budget Pulse is a free online budget planner, whereby you put in all your expenses electronically via an export from your online bank statement. Many other spending trackers exist, but there is a monthly cost for some of them.

If you have a business, it's important to use a software tool to track all expenses and income and follow up late payers.

If any expenses cannot be tracked that way, i.e. you took cash from your purse, you'll need to keep receipts or take notes, and input the transactions manually. Cash spends can really add up so don't let them all slip by. You'll need to do the tracking for at least three months to get any benefit from it.

It's all very easy once you get a handle on the system. However, what's not easy is getting your partner to tell you where he/she spent cash! A category called 'Misc' will be fine for that, if it's only small amounts.

You may find that after using a planner tool, you will no doubt be blown away after tracking everything and doing a 'real life' budget. It was amazing to me that one small family could spend so much in so many different ways, particularly when we are, in general, careful spenders.

The longer you do it, the more your money leak areas will show up; and the totals at the bottom (overall income and expenditure) will explain categorically why you 'just can't save'!

You can also use the Envelope System (or savings sub accounts) and still get to a balanced income/outgoing position.

Manual Budgeting

The Envelope System is a manual method of budgeting where a certain amount of money is put aside monthly for a specific purpose in an envelope labelled appropriately. Then whenever you go to make a purchase, you look in the right envelope to see if there are sufficient funds. If the money is there, go for it. If not, you have three options:

1) you don't make the purchase;

2) you wait until you can allocate more money to that envelope;

3) you sacrifice another category by moving money from its associated envelope.

If you don't spend what's in the envelope this month then the next month's allocation is added, resulting in more money in the envelope waiting. The same is true if you have a savings account allocated for Holidays & Gifts, or Home Maintenance.

_____

Savings are Crucial. You might wonder where savings comes into it when rearranging your budget. YOU have to put it in as an expense!

If possible, aim to allocate say 5% savings and 5% voluntary Super (retirement fund) from your monthly budget... although this allocation depends on your age and situation. It's important that Mums and Dads not only save for the kids, but also save for their own futures. Scott Pape of the Barefoot Investor, calls this amount 'mojo money'.

'Holidays' is a category that often proves a bit problematic. You will need to allocate it a monthly budget, however in one or two months of the year it will look crazy in the budget as you spend that allocation. If you're not in the habit of 'saving up' for a holiday, instead feeling the pain of credit card spending after-wards, you really must try this method. (Some of you will have to ignore those impulse holiday break ideas, sorry).

After working all year you will need and deserve a holiday, espe-cially one that you have saved for. It is important for your mental health!

Take out a new bank account or online saver sub-account spe-cifically for one-off saving amounts. If you've done every other budget category accurately and not left too many unknowns, and you've got an emergency fund slowly building (more on this in Pillar 3), you should know what you have left over for holidays and gifts. It won't be as much as you'd like, probably. Relatives, you might have to receive some gifts of jam and hand-sewn wares!

But anyway, say it's $4,000 per year, or $333 per month. Have an automatic direct debit set to transfer $333 out of your everyday account once a month. (This is once you've ensured your budget has room for it and you're not debt trapped).

Tip 1: Holidays often coincide with Christmas, so put them together in your savings sub-account. Put a small amount aside and try to start in January, or decide how much you need and divide by how long you've got to save up.

Tip 2: Don't forget birthday presents in your budget and include for spouses an agreed amount to spend. (It's fairer if you both have a similar amount, despite who earned the main income).

RELATIONSHIP MONEY TASKS

In most life partnerships, but not all, there is someone more focused on income earning, and someone more focused on household budget and cost cutting. So while this may not work for everyone, I focus on balancing the budget, finding better deals, making monthly bill repayments, and ensuring planned savings are put aside into a different account.

Having learnt that some people will just leave the bills until the red letters come, let's say I'm well aware that arranging the household financial details are my thing. I am a saver. You might find this is reversed in your household, so I'm not saying it's a female role to handle the household finances. Naturally, though, us regular shoppers may be more accustomed to budgeting variable expenses. So we will perhaps find it the easiest to create a budget or use the app and check it regularly. The person who does most of the shopping should always be aware of the budget.

Regardless, it's a good idea for the other partner to check the budget amounts too, so they can keep that in mind when buying discretionary items. The important thing is not to nag your partner. Simply ask the questions that have to be asked, and if he or she is curious, show them the screen with the monthly bar chart of how your budget is doing. Is it maxed out? This graph really is worth a thousand words.

Ensure you fill in the "Assets" and "Liabilities" (mortgage) section – then it will give you a Net Worth figure. This is impressive for your partner to see and for you to keep reinforcing in your mind the growth of your overall net worth.

A budget is not to be used to control the other person! Responsibly knowing your budget and the reasons for budgeting is important for both partners. It is a good thing. Even the kids can learn of their toys or after-school lessons budget—at the same time learning that endless money doesn't come from those holes in the wall. When you add a new activity, the child can have a say in which no-longer-loved activity can be dropped.

CUTTING EXPENSES

Often we don't look at our everyday bills and question them enough. I've found some people are on monthly internet and phone bundle plans that are now $20 dearer than current deals (same company) but with less bandwidth features!

Insurance is an area that is difficult to assess just by cost. If renewing, look at what your home/contents or car insurance really covers for, and see if comparative policies are less or more.

Shop around online with the comparison sites. Here are some of the main ones:

www.canstar.com.au – Compare insurance, home loans, business loans, car loans, bank accounts, investing products, and read helpful articles.

www.choice.com.au – Paid-for reports/reviews on top providers of insurance and consumer products.

www.google.com – "**compare autoinsurance**" (USA - auto)

www.moneysupermarket.com/mortgages/ (for UK)

www.bankrate.com/ (USA – compare mortgages, bank rates, credit cards, insurances, and retirement calculators).

Tip: Go look at your bank statements and add up the monthly fees for transactions. Then add up the fees and interest on any credit cards or store cards on a monthly basis. Also check the annual fee. This is how the banks make billions in profit—so reduce your ATM transactions if your bank charges fees and reduce your number of credit cards.

You can live without credit cards, especially if you get a debit card with Visa or Mastercard logo. These days that's all you need, but if you're still concerned about getting a solid credit record, then a small personal loan is much easier to self-discipline.

PILLAR 2: ERADICATE PERSONAL DEBT

Look at a debt situation from a wider perspective. All your life you will have to pay bills and you'll need to earn income. Perhaps this time you've 'gone over', with less income than expenses, but there are many ways to take the pressure off.

Here are some of the ideas that financial counsellors in Australia may offer:

- Consolidate your high interest loans into one lower interest loan or mortgage (be mindful of the sharks)

- Ask for more time to pay, or pay debt off by instalments.

- Renegotiate your repayments to reduce them and either cover all interest charged, or ask for an interest freeze for a period.

- Place a moratorium on payments (stop for 2 months, or identify when you will be able to resume paying when your situation changes).

- Increase your income by selling old things on online classifieds, or by direct selling with party plan or Avon˙. If you have a blog, you could become an advertising affiliate for an established company. (But be careful not to be suckered into some network marketing/multi-level marketing promises that you're going to become rich).

- Work off debt to friends and family by doing odd jobs (arrange an hourly credit amount).

- If it's a loan of some kind, apply for hardship variations through the Consumer Credit Code.

Last resort: apply to access personal superannuation, if all debt outstanding seems un-repayable given your situation.

CREDIT CARD TRAPS

It seems that there is a small minority of people who can actually make monthly personal borrowings work for them, i.e. always paying their whole credit balance in full every month. The rest of us (including my younger self) get into the whole vicious cycle of living just a bit beyond our means and never quite knowing where we are, financially speaking.

There is also no such thing as free credit. Consider these fees and drawbacks:

- Zero % Balance transfer? Look for the 'Balance Transfer Handling fee' and annual fees once established.

- Annual credit card fees range from $39 to $99 or more, and they are not refunded pro-rata if you switch credit cards to another provider.

- Overlimit fees when your maximum limit is breached (range

from $9 to $20 for accounts opened before 9 June 2012 or to those who agree to over-limit by written consent). NAB do not charge at all.

- Late payment fees if minimum payment is not made by the second or third day after the due date (now reduced only because of the banking Royal Commission). You can avoid this fee by using Autopay.

- Interest payable straightaway on cash advances.

- Interest payable on total—regardless of interest-free period —if you have not paid off the last month's balance. (This does not apply to all credit types, so check yours).

So, here is my advice:

Pay off the highest interest debt/s first, unless it is a major sum. In this case, knock off the smaller credit cards or loans and then cancel them. This gives you a sense of making headway. Ensure ongoing payments are sustainable, so that you are not living just on beans for the week because you paid down your debt.

ASAP, swap your credit cards and store cards for Debit Visa or Debit Mastercard. Yes, you can also keep a credit card in credit balance but there is little benefit and much temptation. These debit cards can be used online and in stores by using the 'credit' button (unless you want cash out). Rather than borrowing, you must ensure there is money in the account first. Seek a good credit union, building society or community bank near you that offers this.

Pay off any family or friends' loans on an agreed direct transfer payment plan. Repaying their generosity and regaining their trust is more important than a lot of the little things you might spend it on.

Pay off any home mortgage a little faster by making one extra payment per year (i.e. split your monthly payment into two fortnightly) on a Principal & Interest loan, or by linking a 100% offset account.

It is important to NOT have an EFTPOS card attached to the offset account, for the sake of the mortgage. Put all your salaries direct into the offset or transfer monthly, and then redraw a living amount each week. Keeping a healthy balance in the offset means this will be reducing the monthly interest on that portion. It's small, but easy to do.

If you have a 'payday' loan, perhaps seek the advice of a counsellor and definitely pay it out as quickly as possible. The interest rates are sky high and keep you from getting ahead.

PROBLEMS PAYING YOUR MORTGAGE?

In Australia, after one year of paying a mortgage, if you hit a spot of trouble you can apply to your financer for a three-month to six-month 'financial hardship' payment holiday. This is more for a Principal and Interest style loan. Alas, you will have to pay it all back and interest still accrues on your overall debt, and so increases your total repayable amount for the future.

You can also ask for payments to be readjusted over a longer time frame. Ask to speak to the financial hardships officer at your lender.

If you have money available in a redraw or offset account, then work out a tight monthly budget to live off this amount while looking for income solutions. Be aware of the debt climbing back up and determine when it will reach the maximum 95%. (Remember, you may not be able to apply for a loan to use your home equity if you don't have a regular job or solid business with annual statements).

A last-ditch effort for those heavily in debt and avoiding bankruptcy is to apply for hardship access to your Superannuation. Ensure you have a financial counsellor go over your options before applying, as this is a serious step backwards.

If your partner runs off on you, leaving you with a bunch of debt and an impending divorce, also consult with a Legal Aid professional.

At no time should you ring up a temporary loan service or debt consolidation service after seeing an advert on the TV or Internet.

CONSOLIDATING DEBT

Many people heavily in debt consolidate their personal car and credit card loans into their home loan, which is always at a much lower interest rate. This requires a "refinance" application, often with a new lender. Before you do this, consider the following.

Each move may cost something, so perhaps check if there is any exit fees from finance lenders. Fixed interest loans can incur a cost called 'a break cost'. Another thing to remember is: if you don't change your habits, your debt is ballooning and not being paid down.

You will want to look for a flexible lender with a low interest rate, low or nil fees, and flexible features like free redraws or an offset account. A good finance broker will inform you of all the fees and charges and aid you with your new application.

You would still need to pass lender credit checks and income checks, so if you are newly unemployed there are other options to pursue. You will need to have at least a 12-month good track record with payments on your loans. Lenders avoid high risks, and people who miss payments on their loans are considered a high risk. Also ensure that with your current monthly income after tax (whether joint or single) your new repayments would be less than or equal to 30%. Don't count overtime payments.

Do a budget plan with your new repayment in mind, and ensure that you will not overspend again, by writing yourself some 'money management rules'. Knowing exactly how much you spend each month and where your blowouts often lie will help your financial future tremendously.

THE UPSIDE OF DEBT REDUCTION

I feel we need some cheering up, so let's look at the positives of paying out debt in an orderly fashion. The main thing is, quickly paying out your debts means that in future (providing your income remains the same) you won't really miss a substantial amount of your cash. Furthermore, after this personal debt is paid, the money can go towards your next savings targets.

Let's take the example of Hunter (28), who is employed as a painter and is single. He currently owes around $17,000 in personal debt, incurred for a car loan (remainder) and some credit card purchases when he moved.

	INTEREST RATE	YEARLY COST OF HAVING THIS LOAN	CURRENT MONTHLY RE-PAYMENT
Car loan for $17,000, now at $13,000	8.69%	$821.25 + application fees	$420.55 (over 4 years)
Bank credit card (rewards), average balance $4,000	19.99%	$799.60 + $100 annual fee = $899.60	$80 (paying the 2% minimum)

* Based on Westpac Altitude card, has $100 fee, but rewards of $100 is applied if you spend more than $8,400 p.a. Assumed that he didn't make the required spending.

Wow! He didn't realise until he worked it out on average, that lending instead of saving up costs him about $1745 per year! Before, it didn't seem very much compared to some people, but now he knows it's a saving stopper.

On checking all the rates at **infochoice.com.au**, Hunter finds the car loan still looks a competitive rate, so he leaves that at the current repayment. But he knows the credit card is keeping him from saving, so his new repayment plan that is doable according to his budget is: $380 per month.

If Hunter stops buying on credit, he will be all clear within 13 months, and this amount includes for interest and fees.

Second year of plan:

In his new budget (without any credit or store card), Hunter wants to save up for a Tinny (that's a little tin boat) that is $4,500 or so. So he decides to speed up his repayments on his car, as he is managing to pay all his other expenses. He now has $10,093 to go (or two years), but if he pays $881 per month he will pay the car out in 12 months. Hunter decides cutting back is worth it.

What You Own	−	What You Owe	=	Net Worth

Third year:

What a pain that loan has been, Hunter thinks. Now he is rid of the credit card repayment and the car loan, Hunter sets a target to save $20,000 towards a boat and his next vehicle. He does this by saving $600 per month in an automatic direct transfer to an online saver.

So he sets up a UBank Usaver (a nil fee online savings account) with 2.31% interest, and expects to save up $20,000 (dependent on interest rates) in 2.75 years. (By then his 'new' car will be five years old, yet it will still retain some value to trade).

––––––––––

Although this is just an example, this example contains guidelines for setting a target, using automatic transfers in line with budgeting, and debt reduction of high interest loans.

These are called 'short term goals'. But what about the long-term goals of paying off a house, investing in property, and retirement saving? This all goes on a written plan.

PILLAR 3: PERSONAL FINANCE PLANNING

When your financial life is in turmoil, I've found that creating order helps. Creating a typed financial life plan for our family, we outlined our income targets, home mortgage repayment goals, retirement savings targets, education savings allocation for our daughter, life insurance protection needed, and wills/estate planning. So this is more personal than your regular adviser-written financial plan.

Every six months, we jointly review the plan again, with current circumstances in mind. What follows is advice drawn from my own financial learning or experience.

Monthly Chunking. When you have a big money goal, break it down into manageable monthly chunks, just as we did in the debt reduction example. It's much easier to save $75 per month for 3 years than come up with $3,000 at once.

Time Horizon. Remember to think about how long you want to keep those savings safe for. For example, if you have 10 years to save for your child's tertiary studies, but feel that equities are too uncertain, then look at term deposits, 10-year insurance bonds, or a well-diversified ETF (Exchange Traded Fund). A financial adviser (say with your credit union) may help you decide the best route.

Financial Statements. You also need to track and adjust your assets and liabilities. Any time you add money to bank accounts, RSAs/Super, put funds under management, buy property, etc, these go onto the plan under 'Current Assets'. Similarly, loans or outstanding credit will go under 'Current Liabilities'.

Current Assets, including cash in bank accounts, less total debts = **your net worth.**

Benefits of a Financial Life Plan

A financial life plan makes it easy to check your progress monthly and your total net worth every year. (You may also use BudgetPulse for basic net worth calculation).

Doing this progress check is very important, as it sets off a deeper motivation to keep with it when see your plans coming along nicely.

For complex or high-net-worth plans, it's advisable to plan together with a financial advisor. It's just that most low and middle-income earners don't see financial advisors regularly.

Whoops—The Stockmarket Went Down!

Even when your equities or other asset takes a short-term dive, if you keep firmly focused on your set goals and the long-term view, you should be able to summon the strength to ride out temporary setbacks. But if you don't trust you can stick with your plan, then you will need a regular financial coach/advisor.

EMERGENCY PLANNING

As soon as you're out of one financial mess, it's important to start planning for the next! So an emergency fund should form a crucial part of your financial plan. Whether it's just one month's salary tucked into an online saver, or the recommended three months' expenses accruing in a mortgage redraw account, this fund gives you the security of having something to come and go on when suffering a job loss, sudden serious illness, or other life-changing situations.

PLANNING FOR WOMEN

Sudden death or divorce can be a devastating financial, not to mention emotional event for many women. Mothers often take a step out of the workforce to care for their children and home, and seem to then have inferior earning-power, and consequently, less money goes into their personal Super accounts.

While we don't like to think of planning for life without our loved one, a few small measures like getting a bank account in your name and saving up some part-time income all helps to ensure starting funds will be there if something bad does happen.

If Divorce is looming: if co-owning a house, the proceeds may not become available until after two years' separation, so you'll need to plan out how you'll pay rent and how you'll juggle work and family on a budget.

Unfortunately, single mothers are some of the lowest income earners in our society, but with a good plan you will be much better off.

If you still have young children (under 6) and earn less than $800 fortnightly, Parenting Payment (Centrelink Australia) could help. Perhaps look for flexible alternatives to 9-to-5 jobs, such as freelancing (photography, writing), party plan sales, telesales, telecommuting work, ebay selling, renovating old furniture, etc.

Sometimes neighbourhood centres have school holiday programs, affording cheap childcare and allowing you to work. Family Day Care (from 1 day to 5 days) is also quite affordable.

Gain inspiration from reading about other mums largely on their own who have prospered: Sandy Forster, Dymphna Boholt, Rachel Powers, (Australia), Karen Knowler (UK), Alexis Martin Neely (US). (See 'Millionaire Mums' in our Resources section).

PILLAR 4: PROTECTING

Life always throws you the odd lemon, so prepare to make lemonade! Have an income plan just in case one of you might:

1.　Get very ill (cancer is indiscriminate)

2.　Have a baby and take time off

3.　Need to take time off to care for an elderly relative

4.　Lose a job

5.　Want a divorce

6.　Die unexpectedly

Number 1's prime solution is income protection insurance (IPI), but its uses are limited. This covers about 80% of income (after a waiting period of 30 days+) if you get ill and have time off, but generally not if you lose your job. Also available is critical illness insurance, which is a little better as it would cover stay-at-home mothers, casual workers and the self-employed, as well as traditional 9-to-5 workers. This generally covers people who have a heart attack, stroke, or any type of cancer (but always check individual policies for differences).

If you are made redundant, ensure you don't spend all your redundancy pay on maintaining your lifestyle or paying out debt. I've heard about one lady who was made redundant and thought she'd pick up a job right away. So she continued on spending as before, but alas she went through all her money and her credit as she couldn't find a job for four months. Then she had to seek help to get food because her money simply ran out. (In Australia, unemployment benefits do not get paid until the redundancy money has been used up on living, e.g. seven weeks pay redundancy means you will not get a claim approved until after the eighth week).

We can never plan for all contingencies, so if you are a stay at home parent or on a part-time, low income, then work out some career possibilities in case you do suddenly need a larger income. In your spare hours you could train and brush up your skills in readiness.

One option is to learn how to run a service business. Another option is to do an Open Learning diploma or free Coursera.com course. Get some experience by volunteering. There are many options out there to help you get prepared for a new career or launch a low-capital business.

There are types of credit protection insurance available that will keep paying your credit card or loan out in case of job loss. So, if you have $10,000 or more in personal type debt, look into insurance, as the premiums are small.

Other types of insurance for loss of job or business are:

- Business Expenses insurance.

- Mortgage Protection insurance (this is the voluntary kind, not the compulsory one the bank/lender needs if you borrow more than 80% of the value).

LIFE INSURANCE

We come to the unspoken problem of death in the family. Number 6's preventative solution is life insurance. What it prevents is hardship. A policy of at least $100,000 with your retirement fund is normally viable, as the premiums are very reasonable. That said, make sure you're not paying two lots of premiums if you happen to have two or more retirement funds -- this eats away at your fund total. (Always rollover into the bigger fund).

Payouts can range from $80,000 to $1 million, and the higher payout is normally chosen by the highest earner in the family. Or if you're both on similar income, why not get similar insurance. A minimum payout amount to cater for is: your total debts + 3 months living expenses, less any superannuation fund/retirement payout. (Some insurance brokers work it out differently).

Eg. $220,000 mortgage + $2,300 pm expenses (x 3) − $75,000 retirement fund = $151,900

So in this example you would insure the income earner for a minimum of $152,000, or more if the person left behind is not able to work for a long period.

Speak to your fund's financial planner or insurance broker some more about this, as many people are underinsured or not insured for death of the part-time earner/stay-at-home Mum. And what a busy and varied 'job' that is to cover for!

THERE WILL BE EMERGENCIES

If you have kept an emergency fund, you will be able to survive fine while you prepare for the future, or have a baby, or care for a dying relative. Putting on your "what if" hat now and then, and saving up for emergencies, may help you immeasurably if the unwanted and unexpected does happen.

PILLAR 5: ALWAYS PAY YOURSELF FIRST

This is important. If you're not in crisis, you must save 10% of your after-tax income! (This is after doing Pillar 1). Whether you want to plough most of it into Super, or if younger, save up for a home, it entirely depends on you. With Superannuation, there are tax benefits for salary earners, and for home savers, they can save a massive amount by not paying home loan interest and any Lenders Mortgage Insurance (payable if you don't have 20% deposit).

Paying yourself by automatic direct transfer right after payday is necessary, because you are not allowing yourself to spend all of your discretionary income and then find you cannot save. This is important whatever your wage.

This 10% savings is not to be used for short-term needs or to pay out debts if possible (also see Eradicate Debt, pillar 2). It's long term. Save for any valid reason: for when your toddler goes to college, or for when you do a degree at 80, or for when you want to retire to Tahiti to live. Our personal reasons to save are really important to keep us motivated.

PILLAR 6: GIVING BACK AND TEACHING OTHERS

When we give money to a cause without reciprocation, more comes along to replace it. (This is termed the Law of Giving). You can choose what you want to give, and whom you give it to. Keeping it local is beneficial for your community.

Decide how much to give (5 or 10%) and do it automatically through direct debit.

Keep records for the yearly tax deduction (no-one said you need to pay tax on your giving!)

INCOME RECOVERY THROUGH TEACHING

Another way you can boost your income is by teaching or to write about your gathered knowledge, online. It's fairly easy to set up a hosted website (with SquareSpace, Shopify or Word-Press) and then create masses of content pages over time.

These interesting pages or posts of at least 500 words should relate to your life experiences and learning. In some cases, combined with research and statistics to back it up. Share it all on your social media profiles and get friends to help out here.

Monetize this by:

- Writing an ebook and selling it (advertise it on the sidebar).

- Selling complementary products as an 'affiliate' or 'reseller' (see Clickbank.com, ClixGalore, or just surf around to see if you can find a book line or product line in the field of your passion).

- Putting up relevant companies' ads in your site's sidebar, signing up with Google Adsense, or similar advertising.

- Make a series of videos to sell as an online course. (**YesCourse.com** makes this easier).

- Conduct webinars and invite experts to talk – you could charge your subscribers a fee or educate about an area you actually service. (Get a 'Dummies' book on the topic).

- Once your blog of Instagram account is established, get paid by brands to post opinions on their products.

Be inspired to live your dream life and try out your passion:

Justin Herald took $50 at age 25 and started screen-printing t-shirts. Justin created Attitude Inc, a clothing brand that (with his marketing savvy) became an international licensing success that turned over in excess of $20 million per year.

Exited from this brand, Justin is now a motivational speaker in Australia/NZ and has a passion to help make people successful. I would say that his attitude is quite 'unreasonable'.

Here is a great quote about this attitude:

"The reasonable man adapts himself to the world; the unreasonable one persists in trying to adapt the world to himself. Therefore all progress depends on the unreasonable man."

- George Bernard Shaw (in 1903, they didn't have women in those days…)

Pillar 7a: Prepare to Invest

Once your financial life is more in place and your income is coming in nicely, you will be ready to set goals for investment. However if you are still at rock bottom, before you get mad and slam down this book, read Pillar 7b. It's just for you.

While you are waiting 12 months+ for your savings to mount up, simultaneously you will be learning all about investing, and tracking where we are on the economic clock (e.g. downturn, boom, credit contraction).

Your goals should determine how you invest, more than your general feeling. If you only want to invest for 3 years say, in order to pay for your child's braces, then the options narrow down to steadier and more liquid options. Many people decide to put the savings into their mortgage and redraw it later (although this means re-borrowing).

Keeping your money safe in the bank is the easy option. But for hard-working, hard-saving taxpayers, it's not a wealth building option because there is no leverage and you are taxed on any small amount of interest you might accrue.

Whether you are looking for shares or houses, first determine your investing strategy. For example, it might be important to you that your investment has a good yield (ongoing return).

Don't ever chase speculative investments when starting out. Start off with amounts around $1,000 - $3,000 each in solid mid and large size companies, with good forecasts and solid dividends.

Also do not buy just because of a massive price drop. Look for value, not for debt-ridden, management-heavy companies.

Another way to invest in a variety of companies but with low capital is to get an ETF.

Exchange Traded Funds from providers like iShares, State Street Global, or Russell, allow you to buy into solid high-yielding shares or top ASX200 shares. You simply pay a brokerage fee and low ongoing management fees of 0.5% or similar.

PROPERTY

Or if property is your goal, perhaps start off with getting a hot spot report and then a good wealth accountant's advice on what is the best tax-beneficial type of property for you, at this stage in your life. Don't forget to allow for unforeseen drops in income and interest rate rises up to variable rates of 9 or 10%.

SUPERANNUATION

Superannuation (or 401K) is also a tax-advantageous wealth builder, if you can get yourself past all the disappointing returns.

An actively-managed retirement account is more likely to give you a comfortable retirement. So be an active investor and monitor what your Super is invested in. Does the fund's asset break-up reflect your required risk level and age and stage?

The default for Super funds is the Balanced option. But does Balanced mean that the cash or fixed interest component is 15%

or 30%? Does it have a lot of exposure to overseas investments? These are generally more likely to have negative growth years. Risk is difficult for the novice to assess, so I suggest you seek some advice from an advisor at your retirement fund.

If it's an industry fund, you could be entitled to free advice on: asset allocations, rollovers, salary sacrifice or personal and government co-contributions, and so on. Why not use the free advice first? You'll probably learn more about what you can do with regard to enhancing your Super's performance.

After age 55 (in Australia), you have the option to draw down a pension from your Super as well as putting salary directly into it, and thus benefiting from a low tax environ. It's called a Transition To Retirement plan.

The tax rate on money going in is 15% and earnings are now also taxed at 15%. There are caps (limits) on what you can put in every year to get this rate, so check the latest advice on this too.

After 60, for now you can withdraw from superannuation free of tax. Most people retiring these days set up their own annuity (or self-funded pension) rather than withdraw a lump sum. This certainly makes a lot of sense, but also check that the pension capital is invested in a really diversified fund.

~ ~ ~ ~ ~ ~

So you see, investing is not just for the rich. Starting out armed with research, planning, and a small amount, you can build up from there. Never wait to invest because you fear the first step. As Susan Jeffers said, "feel the fear – and do it anyway".

Also never invest out of greed, such as on a 'hot tip' or a 'friend's surefire business' or a cold calling 'opportunity' or a 'buy off the plan – no money until….', or fall prey to a property developer's huge gain from a hyped-up seminar.

Scamwatch website (**www.scamwatch.gov.au/**) can inform you all about the latest get rich quick schemes and cold calling scams. MoneySmart (**www.moneysmart.gov.au/scams/**) has a list of unlicensed financial companies from around the world.

PILLAR 7B: TAKING ACTION

This section is for those who have no way to invest yet. When you're unemployed or unhappy with a lowly job, you're waiting for an opportunity to prove your worth. This wait may prove disheartening. But when you are making things, writing books, building a business from scratch, or even writing a business plan, you're taking actions towards your goal.

You're making things happen.

So, in the above cases, you assume the power when you take your own ideas and serve an identified market need. In 1999, I couldn't write a book to save myself, but I knew I wanted to write well so I went to University and I took writing and editing classes. Some time later I had an idea for a book about breaking bad spending habits, a theme that I know resonates with other women, and I got to writing my own little book. I then learnt how to self-publish it using 'Lulu.com' and they made my book into an eBook. It started to sell. I was still a freelancer, not a superstar, but with small pushes I made one dream come true. Ever since then, if I thought I had a good idea for a book, some sound knowledge, and a market for that book, I thought 'why not'... rather than 'why me?'

If you want more in life, then the very first step is to know what you want (see 'setting goals'). The next step is to brainstorm ideas.

It is so important to get out of a mental rut (a recurring pattern of thinking), and to do this you need lots and lots of ideas and envisioning. Sounds corny, but you are to become an idea factory.

These ideas will then be checked by Quality Assurance that they align with your values, your personal mission (if applicable) and your physical and mental abilities. (Although don't underestimate yourself – look at what people achieve on The Biggest Loser).

QA doesn't worry if they have not found a childcare option yet. QA does not stop to ring their Mum, Dad or significant other to seek support. (A surefire stopper!) No, your own QA 'decider of which good idea' is best to: find the idea that fires you up, the idea that you believe there is a hungry market for. And if you haven't already heard the same definite need from six to ten people, then market research is your next step.

Market Research can be done in a number of ways:

a) Social – through surveys to interested people/relevant groups.

b) Consumer-purchase based – whereby you put trial advertising, say via eBay listings, and thus determine demand.

c) Trend research – Google Trends helps to compare popular topics, large newspaper websites (the daily items are marked 'most read'), Amazon bestseller lists, and so on, are all tools for trend research.

How to be an Idea Factory

- Turn off your critical assessor

- Each morning, think of 10 – 12 ideas related to your life stage, e.g. 12 lean business ideas, 12 bestseller book titles to write, 12 micro-niches for coaching, or 12 actions to get publicity for a cause. Our mind works better when it's not tired.

- Without wondering 'how', get your QA to assess each idea for feasibility, marketing wise, and relevance to your aims and values. Imagine QA as an independent, positively critical assessor. QA wants the best for you; it is your hidden business mind.

- If you keep coming back to the idea, then look for ways to immerse yourself in it, e.g. being an intern, carrying out surveys, making blueprints, doing a related course, etc.

Trial it before leaping in!

Creative types might make two or three initial crafted products and list them with photos on Etsy (a global online crafter's marketplace), then share in relevant social groups to see how they sell.

Most entrepreneurs with a new product have found consumer purchases to be more reliable testing than feedback and surveys, where there is no commitment required and sometimes a friendship bias is at play.

That said, surveying can uncover new applications for your ideas and determine the most desired features. See **SurveyMonkey. com** for free surveys to send to your network.

See the answers to common financial questions...

FPA (Financial Planning Association of Australia) **http://ask.fpa.com.au/**

Do a financial planning calculation....

MoneySmart (ASIC) calculators for mortgage planning, budgeting and saving, retirement planning, loans/debt repayment, money health calculator, etc.

www.moneysmart.gov.au/tools-and-resources/calculators-and-apps

CHAPTER 6

THE BUSINESS OF STILL BEING IN BUSINESS

Business income trouble feels isolating and stressful, and it can happen to anyone in any economic climate. Even if things are rocky, it's not inevitable that your business will close... if your debts are not insurmountable.

First and most obvious, you need to identify the source of your income woes. Is it cash flow holdups? Poor sales? The wrong type of clients? Is it internal to business, like theft or a lazy partner? Is it you not valuing your own service?

We can't determine the root of every problem, but there are certain things you *must* do to succeed in business. Equally, there are things you must NOT do. Here is a list of things business owners commonly do to create failure -- and their corresponding answer.

1. Don't run three businesses at once and spread yourself too thin. Focus on one good business and one target market and serve this well.

2. Don't sell one product style to diverse, separate markets (it's 'hit and miss' and hard to market to). Create a new product or offering for the same market, to build on your success. This is the 'inch wide and mile deep' theory.

3. Don't offer lots of products on one website and confuse your market. Instead, bundle up lots of your smaller products and offer these bundles at two or three price points. E.g. In an online shop offering 450 promotional products, on the home page offer big and bold "the Corporate Promo Pack" and "the Small Business Promo Pack". It's far easier to choose between two options.

4. Don't spend all your time on the low-end, time-consuming clients. Look for the high-end clients, avoid or 'fire' the time wasters, and spend time/funds over-delivering to the high payers. They also tend to appreciate you more and some of them will give high quality referrals.

5. Don't spend heaps of money in advertising before you test each marketing tactic. A low-cost digital strategy should be planned, along with offline visibility, like car signage, branded t-shirt, and enthusiastic participation at regular networking events. You can also add writing up news that's relevant to your community and emailing it to local news editors. (Stress the local angle).

For in-depth help, see your local Business Enterprise Centre (Australia) or Business.USA.gov/Entreworld (North America).

WHAT'S IN IT FOR ME?

You are not your specialty... People don't care about your title or qualifications; they care about what problems of theirs you can solve.

If you prefer not to spend two weeks doing market research— that is, finding out what the consumers known as 'innovators' want from a business in your niche—then you may as well save yourself lots of time and money pushing it out to a market. After all, if the ones who are obsessed with your topic don't respond, then nobody else will.

I used to just write what I felt was good advice in a book and put it online, with a matching website or sales page. I did this two times. But I had not researched what my market was looking for, and undoubtedly I was using the wrong keywords. So I learnt about keyword research, and more and more about target marketing to a niche. I teamed it with knowledge of consumer behaviour.

A book is a product just like any other product, and needs to be sold to remedy a readership's problems or desires.

Consumers often have a hot 'pain point' that your product, service or affiliate product could solve. If so, then the simple steps you need to take are:

- Find out where those people are hanging out

- Write an emotive headline, and

- Point out the benefits of your solution.

You can even talk about your solution through short videos, a webinar, or podcast. (Plan these so you're not rambling).

You can find out pain points by asking your customers or likely prospects via a survey. This feedback can also form part of new product development. Use **SurveyMonkey.com** for this.

MARKETING YOUR MESSAGE

When you learn the art of copywriting, you learn the most effective way to communicate your message with customers. Having been a copywriter, I recommend you learn this art yourself… if you've got the time and the capacity. It will certainly help you in every facet of business marketing.

Creative copy can be used in print advertising, website pages, article bylines, simple online ads, and direct mailers. A better message will always beat a cool logo. A strong message directed to the hidden desires of your customers will resonate, just like a great news headline captures your attention.

Even though the world is changing fast, the tenets of writing sales-winning copy – and getting to peoples' hearts – never change. Learn through home study courses or books by Bob Bly and Dan Kennedy (two prolific copywiters). If you learn all about marketing, then any business can be your client or employer. You might also use this info to run your own business in a better way.

Check out the Digital Marketing courses at **Coursera.com** or Open Universities... **www.open.edu.au.** We also have marketing courses for new authors at **BusinessAuthorAcademy.com.**

CONCLUSIONS

Don't you hate it when you've read a book and the author says they're now rich and have finished their journey? Well, that's not the end of my story and neither is it the end of this story.

I can, however, share that my emotional state changed to more contentment and less anxious periods when I started to see possibilities and question my limiting beliefs. It improved a little more every time I went back to re-write my goals and refine my vision. It helped to remember my favoured values, and I have no regrets about giving up some regular income in favour of time spent with my special girl. (When I wasn't writing books, that is!)

Since those dark days, our entire situation has improved, in the most part due to an application of 'nose to the grindstone' and choosing a great niche.

I believe that choosing a niche that aligns with what you believe, what you're good with and are passionate about is the cornerstone of attracting abundance and prosperity.

The niche I have chosen is helping authors to produce a book and content that builds on their personal brand. Another niche is teaching soloists and authors digital marketing. I have services or courses that help people within those niches.

It's serendipitous when your life experience joins up with your acquired skills and a passion you have to help. Things start moving in the right direction. So, never let the passion you have wither under your financial stress.

Create your new life of abundance through: goal setting and self-discovery, teaching people in your own niche, managing your money with more conscious thought, and by maintaining a positive mental attitude. You may surprise yourself with how far it takes you!

RESOURCES FOR ASSISTANCE

Prosperity Times **www.prosperitytimes.org**

Or see **www.jenniferlancaster.com.au/blog**.

AUSTRALIAN RESOURCES

Australian hotline for Financial Counselling: 1800 007 007

Financial First Aid line: 1300 370 255

Saver Plus – for parents or students with a Centrelink health care card, saving towards education & training.

www.bsl.org.au/services/money-matters/saver-plus/

Saver Plus assists families on low incomes to develop a savings habit, build assets and improve financial skills through workshops. Participants set a savings goal and receive support to help them achieve it. When they reach their goal, every dollar of their savings are matched by ANZ, up to $500. Matched savings are then spent on costs relating to participants' vocational training or their children's schooling.

Available in Brisbane at The Smith Family: Phone (07) 3115 6228

Lifeline crisis support: 13 11 14

Find Lost Super - **www.superseeker.super.ato.gov.au**

Find Unclaimed Money in your name (accounts, wages, insurance) **www.moneysmart.gov.au/tools-and-resources/find-unclaimed-money**

United States Resources

ACCC Consumer Credit (licensed):
www.consumercredit.com/our-services/credit-counseling.aspx

CareOne Debt Relief (no bankruptcy counsel):
www.careonecredit.com/

Note: Debt counseling should be free. In America, a standard fee to set up a debt management plan is around $50, and the monthly maintenance cost should be no more than $25. (Information from TopTenReviews.com).

Find Unclaimed Money (funds, accounts, wages, DVA, tax refunds)
www.usa.gov/unclaimed-money

UK Resources

Find Unclaimed Assets (dormant accounts, bonds, lotteries)
http://unclaimedassets.co.uk/trace-forgotten-funds/

Books Referred to

Millionaire Mumpreneurs, Mel McGee, 2010, Harriman House. Profiles: Janet Beckers, Karen Knowler, Elizabeth Potts Weinstein, Alexis Martin Neely, Fabienne Fredrickson, Sheri McConnell, and tips for your success.

Turning Passions into Profits, Christopher Howard, 2004, John Wiley & Sons.

REFERENCES

1. The Bankwest Curtin Economics Centre study, June 2015

2. 'Australian Household Debt Triples', ABC News, http://www.abc.net.au/news/2015-06-17/australian-household-debt-triples/6551352

3. *Bounce Forward: How to Transform Crisis into Success*, Sam Cawthorn, 2013, John Wiley & Sons.

4. *Learned Optimism*, Martin E.P. Seligman, 2006 edition, 1st edition published 1990, Random House.

5. *Dying for a Cure*, Rebekah Beddoe, 2007, Random House.

6. *Shining Through – From Grief to Gratitude.* https://sorayasaraswati.com/grief-to-gratitude/

7. 'Neuro-Plasticity and Depression', Stress-Stop Blog. Jim Porter, June 25, 2010. http://www.stressstop.com/blog/read-entry.php?eid=15

8. 'Depression Physically Changes your Brain', by Melissa Malski, Policy. mic. http://mic.com/articles/53157/depression-physically-changes-your-brain-scientists-discover#.BtOtcQyM7

9. 'Positive Thinking, Persistence Pays Off in Job Search: Study', HealthDay. May 3, 2012. http://news.health.com/2012/05/03/positive-thinking-persistence-pay-off-in-job-search-study/

10. *Think and Grow Rich*, Napoleon Hill, 1937. (71st anniversary edition republished by Stuart Zadel).

11. 'Kids Understand the Benefits of Positive Thinking', Psych Central. http://psychcentral.com/news/2011/12/23/kids-understand-benefits-of-positive-thinking/32943.html).

12. Tips from *Nature and Health Magazine*, Oct-Nov 2015.

About the Author

Jennifer Lancaster started copywriting under Power of Words in 2007. After working in marketing and layout from 1990 to 1999, she completed a Communications (Journalism/Media) degree.

Jen has always had an interest in the world of money, wondering why it's so hard to stop shopping ('How to Kick Bad Spending Habits') and what more we could do to help along our wealth ('How to Control your Financial Destiny').

Implementing marketing and effective copywriting for diverse small businesses gave her the idea to write *'Power Marketing: An Aussie Guide to Business Growth'*. Jen has also helped many business authors with publishing their own books and ebooks, and continues to help businesses with creative content writing.

She now runs Business Author Academy and mentors authors.

Creative Ways with Money

Swift talkers, spruikers, Bitcoin clones and work-at-home opportunities' wait to rob you of your potential to create wealth. Australians lost $86 million in 2018 to investment scams.

Read Creative Ways with Money if you want to avoid swindles... and instead learn some creative ways to save, invest, and earn more money on the side.

Because our mind often holds us back from strategic investing, we also take our fears and emotions out of the dark. You'll learn how to overcome negative thoughts to design your life the way you want it to be.

RRP $23.50. **https://jenniferlancaster.com.au/book/creative-ways-with-money/**

Power Marketing

Jennifer Lancaster explores over 60 ideas for marketing your small business or online enterprise. To save you from costly or ineffective advertising, this book explains how to create a distinctive edge through thought leadership and business writing.

eBook ISBN: 9781311298959 (2015) $4.99 USD.

Print ISBN (2016): 978-0-9804112-8-7

RRP $20.95 AUD (3rd edition). Buy direct at **www.powerofwords.com.au/books**

How to Control Your Financial Destiny

If you want to achieve financial independence at any age, there are some important things you need to know right now. Jennifer Lancaster explains the principles of saving and investing clearly and simply. She urges you to create your own financial plan and budget. It's in your hands, not that of a financial planner, property spruiker, or broker.

ebook ISBN (ibooks): 9780980411256 (2015)
$4.99 USD